Welcome Baby

9 Adorable Quilt Patterns

Welcome Baby: 9 Adorable Quilt Patterns

© 2015 by Martingale & Company®

Martingale

19021 120th Ave. NE, Ste. 102

Bothell, WA 98011-9511 USA

ShopMartingale.com

Printed in China

20 19 18 17 16 15   8 7 6 5 4 3 2 1

Library of Congress Cataloging-in-Publication Data is available upon request.

ISBN: 978-1-60468-573-2

Projects in this book have previously been published in: *Cuddle Me Quick* by Christine Porter and Darra Williamson; *Seamingly Scrappy* by Rebecca Silbaugh; *Quilts Made with Love* by Rachel Griffith; *Quilts from Sweet Jane* by Sue Pfau; *Large-Block Quilts* by Victoria L. Eapen; and *Modern Baby.*

Mission Statement

Dedicated to providing quality products and service to inspire creativity.

Contents

Fresh as a Daisy

A color scheme reminiscent of daisies on a summer morning suggested the name of this cheerful little quilt, and a charming daisy quilting motif reinforces the theme. It's the perfect choice for a new quilter.

Designed, made, and machine quilted by Christine Porter

Quilt size: 32⅜" x 38¾" • **Block size:** 4½" x 4½"

Materials

Yardage is based 42"-wide fabric.

1 yard of blue tone-on-tone for setting triangles
  and binding
⅝ yard *total* of assorted blue prints for blocks
½ yard *total* of assorted yellow prints for blocks
⅜ yard *each* of 2 blue-and-white prints for blocks*
1⅓ yards of fabric for backing
37" x 43" piece of batting

*If you prefer a scrappier look, you can use more than 2
blue-and-white fabrics. You can even substitute twenty
5" charm squares for this yardage.*

Cutting

*Measurements include ¼" seam allowance. Cut all strips
on the crosswise grain (from selvage to selvage).*

From the assorted yellow prints, cut a *total* of:
7 strips, 2" x 42"

From the assorted blue prints, cut a *total* of:
8 strips, 2" x 42"

From *each* blue-and-white print, cut:
2 strips, 5" x 42"; crosscut into 10 squares, 5" x 5"
  (20 total)

From the blue tone on tone, cut:
2 strips, 9" x 42"; crosscut into 5 squares, 9" x 9". Cut
  each square into quarters diagonally to make a
  total of 20 setting triangles (2 are extra).*
2 squares, 5½" x 5½"; cut each square in half
  diagonally to make a total of 4 corner triangles*
4 strips, 2½" x 42"

*These triangles are cut oversized; you'll trim them after
completing the quilt top.*

Making the Blocks

1 With right sides together, sew a 2"-wide yellow
  strip between two 2"-wide assorted blue strips;
press. Make three scrappy strip sets. Cut the strip
sets into a total of 60 segments, 2" wide.

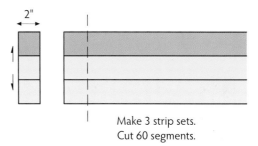

Make 3 strip sets.
Cut 60 segments.

2 With right sides together, sew a 2"-wide blue
  strip between two 2"-wide assorted yellow strips;
press. Make two scrappy strip sets. Cut the strip
sets into a total of 30 segments, 2" wide.

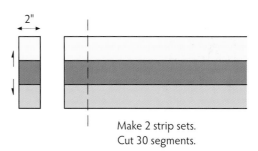

Make 2 strip sets.
Cut 30 segments.

3 Sew a segment from step 2 between two
  segments from step 1; press. Repeat to make 30
scrappy blocks.

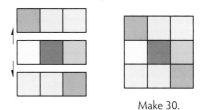

Make 30.

Assembling the Quilt Top

Do not trim the oversized setting triangles until instructed to do so in step 3.

1 Arrange the blocks, the blue-and-white 5" squares, the side setting triangles, and the corner setting triangles in diagonal rows as shown in the quilt assembly diagram below, alternating the placement of the two different 5" squares.

2 Sew the blocks, the squares, and the side setting triangles together into diagonal rows. Sew the rows together. Add the corner triangles. Press as indicated by the arrows after each step.

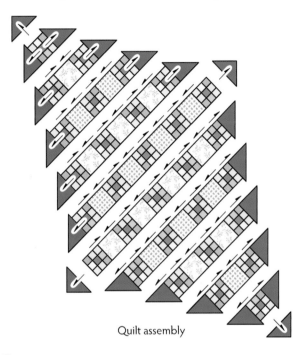

Quilt assembly

3 Carefully straighten the edges of the quilt top by trimming the excess fabric, leaving a generous ¼" from the outer corners of the blocks. Square the quilt corners.

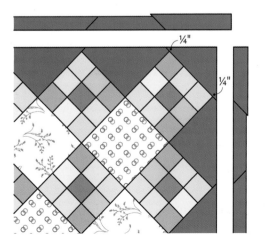

Finishing the Quilt

For more information on finishing techniques, go to ShopMartingale.com/HowtoQuilt for free illustrated instructions.

1 Prepare the quilt backing.

2 Layer the quilt top, batting, and backing; baste the layers together.

3 Hand or machine quilt as desired.

4 Trim the backing and batting even with the quilt top, and then use the blue tone-on-tone 2½"-wide strips to bind your quilt. Add a label and sleeve if desired.

Quilt layout

Bubbles

Dig into your scraps for this quirky and fun baby quilt. Different color choices for the background and the patchwork fish will completely transform the look.

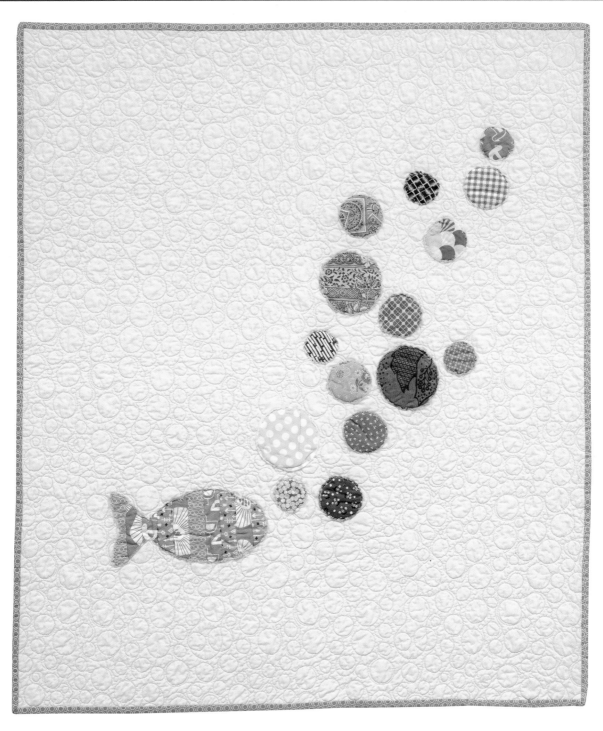

Designed and pieced by Dana Bolyard; machine quilted by Russ Adams of the Back Porch Quilters

Quilt size: 36" x 42"

Materials

Yardage is based on 42-wide fabric unless noted otherwise.

1 yard of pale-aqua solid for background
15 scraps, at least 5" x 5", of assorted blue fabrics for bubbles
11 scraps, at least 1½" x 7", of assorted orange fabrics for fish
⅜ yard of orange print for binding
1⅜ yards of fabric for backing
42" x 48" piece of batting
Template plastic

Cutting

A ¼" seam allowance is included in all measurements unless otherwise specified. Patterns are on page 10. Trace the patterns onto template plastic and cut out; use the templates to cut fabric pieces as directed. Do not add seam allowances to these raw-edge appliqué pieces.

From the assorted blue fabrics, cut:
3 using pattern A
7 using pattern B
5 using pattern C

From the assorted orange fabrics, cut:
11 rectangles, 1½" x 7"

From the orange print, cut:
5 strips, 2¼" x 42"

Hold Steady

Starch is your friend! Using a quality spray starch on the orange strip set will not only yield straighter strips, but also provide more body and stability as you cut out the fish shape.

Assembling the Quilt Top

1 Sew the 11 orange rectangles together side by side along their long edges. Press the seam allowances in one direction.

2 Using the fish pattern on page 10, trace and cut one fish shape from the strip set.

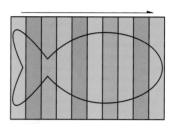

3 Press the aqua background fabric to remove wrinkles and creases, and then pin the strip-pieced fish to the background fabric about 5½" from the left side and 8½" above the bottom edge.

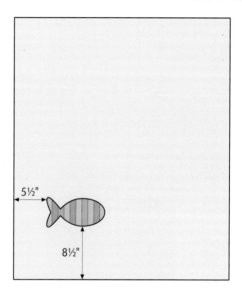

4 Using either a short straight stitch or a zigzag stitch on your machine, sew ⅛" inside the raw edges of the fish. Backtack at the beginning and end.

5 Position the bubbles on the background fabric, referring to the illustration below and the quilt photo on page 7 for placement suggestions. Attach the bubbles in the same manner you used for the fish appliqué.

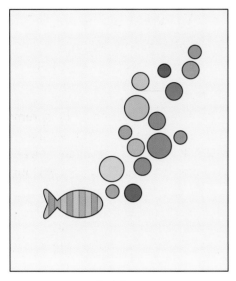

Quilt layout

Finishing the Quilt

For more information on finishing techniques, go to ShopMartingale.com/HowtoQuilt for free illustrated instructions.

1 Prepare the quilt backing.

2 Layer the quilt top, batting, and backing; baste the layers together.

3 Hand or machine quilt as desired. The sample quilt features a continuous-line quilting pattern of small circles that echo the appliquéd bubbles.

4 Trim the backing and batting even with the quilt top, and then use the orange 2¼"-wide strips to bind the edges of the quilt. Add a label and sleeve if desired.

5 Wash the finished quilt to remove all starch residue and to fray the edges of the appliqués.

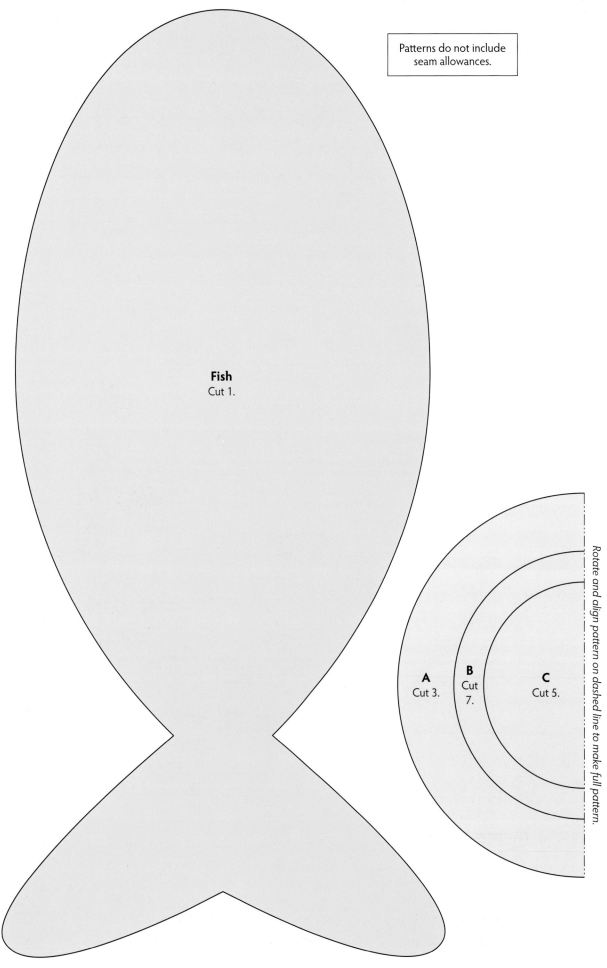

Patterns do not include seam allowances.

Fish
Cut 1.

A
Cut 3.

B
Cut 7.

C
Cut 5.

Rotate and align pattern on dashed line to make full pattern.

Little Sailor

This jaunty, nautical-themed quilt is perfect for cuddling your little sailor now, and for transitioning later to a coverlet for the big-boy or big-girl bed. Rather than cutting triangles, the super-simple sew-and-flip technique is used.

Designed and made by Darra Williamson; machine quilted by Christine Porter

Quilt size: 50" x 60" • **Block sizes:** Sailboat, 8" x 6"; Waves, 8" x 4"

Materials

Yardage is based on 42"-wide fabrics.

1½ yards *total* of assorted light and medium bright prints for Sailboat blocks*

1⅛ yards *total* of assorted medium and dark bright prints for Sailboat blocks*

1⅛ yards *total* of assorted dark-blue prints for Wave blocks**

1⅛ yards *total* of assorted light-blue prints for Wave blocks**

1 yard of blue-green print for outer border

½ yard of multicolored plaid for binding

3⅛ yards of fabric for backing (horizontal seam)

54" x 64" piece of batting

5¾ yards of ½"-wide white-with-yellow rickrack

Matching thread for stitching rickrack

You can substitute twenty-five 5" charm squares (trimmed to 4½") and 2½"-wide precut strips for yardage.

**You can substitute 2½"-wide precut strips for yardage.*

Cutting

Measurements include ¼" seam allowances. Cut all strips on the crosswise grain (from selvage to selvage).

From the medium and dark bright prints, cut a *total* of:

25 squares, 4½" x 4½"

25 rectangles, 2½" x 8½"

From the light and medium bright prints, cut a *total* of *25 matching sets* of the following:

1 square, 4½" x 4½"

2 rectangles, 2½" x 4½"

2 squares, 2½" x 2½"

From the dark-blue prints, cut a *total* of:

50 rectangles, 2½" x 4½"

100 squares, 2½" x 2½"

From the light-blue prints, cut a *total* of:

50 rectangles, 2½" x 4½"

100 squares, 2½" x 2½"

From the blue-green print, cut:

6 strips, 5¼" x 42"

From the multicolored plaid, cut:

6 strips, 2½" x 42"

Making the Sailboat Blocks

For each block, chose one set of matching pieces for the background. You'll need a 4½" square, two 2½" x 4½" rectangles, and two 2½" squares. You'll also need one contrasting 4½" square for the sail and a 2½" x 8½" rectangle for the boat.

1 Draw a diagonal line from corner to corner on the wrong side of a 4½" background square. Place the marked square right sides together with a 4½" contrasting square. Sew directly on the marked line. Trim, leaving a ¼" seam allowance; press.

2 Sew the unit from step 1 between two matching 2½" x 4½" background rectangles; press.

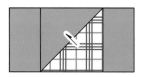

3 Use the sew-and flip method as follows to make the boat: Place a background 2½" square on one end of a 2½" x 8½" contrasting rectangle. Sew diagonally from the top outer corner to the bottom inner corner as shown. Trim, leaving a ¼" seam allowance, and press. Repeat on the other end of the rectangle as shown.

4 Sew the units from steps 2 and 3 together; press. Repeat steps 1–4 to make a total of 25 Sailboat blocks.

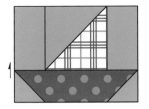

Make 25.

Making the Wave Blocks

1 Using the sew-and-flip method, sew a light-blue 2½" square to one end of a dark-blue 2½" x 4½" rectangle; trim and press. Sew a different light-blue 2½" square to the other end of the rectangle; trim and press. Make two.

Make 2.

2 Sew the two units from step 1 together side by side; press.

3 Sew a dark-blue 2½" square to one end of a light-blue 2½" x 4½" rectangle; trim and press. Sew a different dark-blue 2½" square to the other end of the rectangle; trim and press. Make two and sew them side by side; press.

4 Sew the units from steps 2 and 3 together as shown above right; press.

5 Repeat steps 1–4 to make a total of 25 Wave blocks.

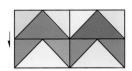

Make 25.

Assembling the Quilt Top

1 Arrange five Sailboat and five Wave blocks *each* in five vertical rows, alternating the Sailboat and Wave blocks as shown in the quilt assembly diagram below. Three rows start with sailboats; two rows begin with waves.

2 Sew the blocks together into vertical rows; press. Sew the rows together; press.

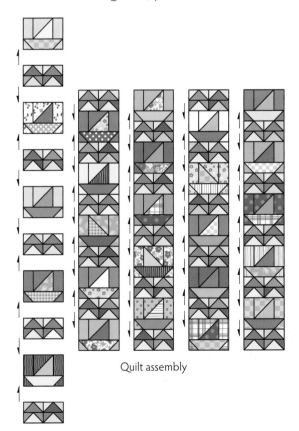

Quilt assembly

3 Sew the blue-green 5¼"-wide strips together end to end using diagonal seams to make one long strip. Measure the quilt through the center from top to bottom and cut two strips to this measurement. With right sides together, sew the strips to the sides of the quilt. Press the seam allowances toward the border.

4 Measure the quilt through the center from side to side, including the borders you've just added. From the remaining blue-green strip, cut two strips to this measurement and sew them to the top and bottom of the quilt; press.

Finishing the Quilt

For more information on finishing techniques, go to ShopMartingale.com/HowtoQuilt for free illustrated instructions.

1 Prepare the quilt backing.

2 Layer the quilt top, batting, and backing; baste the layers together.

3 Hand or machine quilt the center of the quilt as desired; stop when you reach the outer border.

4 Referring to the photo on page 11, place the rickrack on the border, all around the perimeter of the quilt center, directly over the border seam. Fold the rickrack at each corner as necessary to achieve a smooth turn. Trim the excess rickrack, leaving an overlap of approximately 1". Pin generously to secure the rickrack to the quilt. Using matching thread, sew through the center of the rickrack to secure it to the quilt.

5 Quilt the outer border as desired.

6 Trim the backing and batting even with the quilt top, and then use the plaid 2½"-wide strips to bind your quilt, incorporating a label and sleeve.

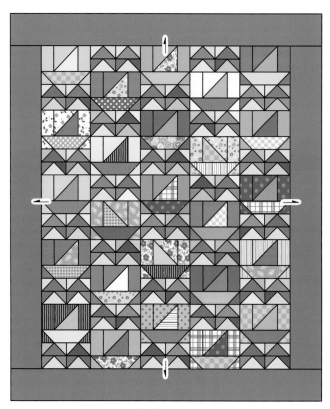

Quilt layout

Cross Weave

A two-color but scrappy quilt is a fun way to play with visual textures and shades rather than color contrast. This simple pattern creates a visually stimulating design for babies.

Designed and made by Amy Smart

Quilt size: 41½" x 47" • **Block size:** 5½" x 5½"

Materials

Yardage is based on 42"-wide fabric unless noted otherwise.

1⅜ yards of white solid for blocks and outer border

21 squares, 5" x 5", of assorted red or pink prints for blocks

6 strips, 2½" x 42", of assorted red or pink prints for blocks*

⅝ yard of pink dot for inner border and binding

2⅝ yards of fabric for backing

47" x 52" piece of batting

More can be used for a scrappier look.

Cutting

Measurements include ¼" seam allowances.

From the white solid, cut:

3 strips, 5" x 42"; crosscut into 21 squares, 5" x 5". Cut in half diagonally to yield 42 triangles.

6 strips, 2½" x 42"; crosscut into 21 rectangles, 2½" x 9"

4 strips, 3½" x 42"; crosscut into 2 strips, 3½" x 41", and 2 strips, 3½" x 41½"*

From the assorted strips, cut a *total* of:

21 rectangles, 2½" x 9"

From the pink dot, cut:

2 strips, 1½" x 39"

2 strips, 1½" x 35½"

5 strips, 2¼" x 42"

Cut a 5th strip and piece the borders, if necessary.

Making the Blocks

1 Fold a white triangle in half and finger-press the long edge at the fold to mark the center point. Repeat with a second white triangle. Fold a print 2½" x 9" rectangle in half and finger-press at the fold to mark the center point on each long edge of the rectangle. Sew the white triangles to opposite sides of the rectangle, aligning the center points. Press the seam allowances toward the rectangle.

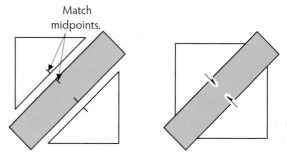

Match midpoints.

2 Square and trim each block to 6" x 6". Make 21.

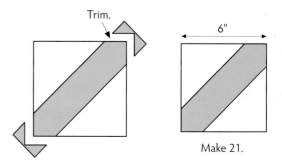

Trim.

6"

Make 21.

3 Cut each assorted print square in half diagonally to create 2 triangles (42 total). Repeat steps 1 and 2, pairing print triangles with white rectangles. Press the seam allowances toward the print triangles. Make 21.

6"

Make 21.

Assembling the Quilt Top

1 Arrange the blocks in seven rows of six blocks each, alternating white-triangle blocks and print-triangle blocks.

2 Sew the blocks together into rows, pressing seam allowances in alternating directions from row to row.

3 Sew the rows together. Press the seam allowances in one direction.

4 Stitch a pink-dot 1½" x 39" inner-border strip to each side of the quilt top. Press the seam allowances toward the border strips. Add the pink-dot 1½" x 35½" strips to the top and bottom edges. Press the seam allowances toward the border strips.

5 Sew a white 3½" x 41" strip to each side of the quilt top. Add the white 3½" x 41½" strips to the top and bottom edges. Press the seam allowances toward the outer borders.

Finishing the Quilt

For more information on finishing techniques, go to ShopMartingale.com/HowtoQuilt for free illustrated instructions.

1 Prepare the quilt backing.

2 Layer the quilt top, batting, and backing; baste the layers together.

3 Hand or machine quilt as desired.

4 Trim the backing and batting even with the quilt top, and then use the pink-dot 2¼"-wide strips to bind the edges of the quilt. Add a label and sleeve if desired.

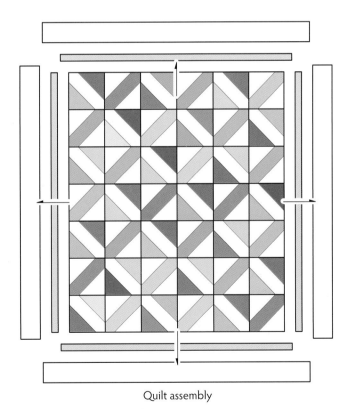

Quilt assembly

Busy Blocks

Vivid solids are a great choice for a baby quilt. The bold colors grow with the child and keep this quilt in use for years! Use the solid fabrics to showcase unique machine quilting in each block.

Designed and made by Shea Henderson

Quilt size: 46" x 46" • Unit size: 3½"

Materials

Yardage is based on 42"-wide fabric and includes fabric for a pieced backing as instructed on page 20.

1 yard of green solid for blocks and backing (fabric A)
1 yard of navy solid for blocks and binding (fabric C)
¾ yard of bright-green solid for blocks (fabric D)
⅝ yard of bright-blue solid for blocks (fabric B)
¼ yard *each* of 4 assorted solids for block centers
    (Choose fabrics in the same color families but
    lighter values than the block fabrics; these are
    fabrics 1–4.)
½ yard of white solid for blocks
2 yards of fabric for backing
52" x 52" piece of batting

Cutting

Measurements include ¼" seam allowances.

From *each* of fabrics A–C, cut:
3 strips, 4" x 42"; crosscut into 20 squares, 4" x 4"
    (60 total)
2 strips, 4½" x 42"; crosscut into 10 squares,
    4½" x 4½" (30 total; 1 B square will be extra)
5 strips, 2¼" x 42", *from fabric C only*

From fabric D, cut:
4 strips, 4" x 42"; crosscut into 28 squares, 4" x 4"
    (reserve 4 for pieced backing)
2 strips, 4½" x 42"; crosscut into 13 squares,
    4½" x 4½"

From *each* of fabrics 1–3, cut:
1 strip, 4" x 42"; crosscut into 6 squares, 4" x 4"
    (18 total)

From fabric 4, cut:
1 strip, 4" x 42"; crosscut into 8 squares, 4" x 4"
    (reserve 1 for pieced backing)

From the white solid, cut:
3 strips, 4" x 42"; crosscut into 24 squares, 4" x 4"

Making the Blocks

1 Stack the 4½" squares in pairs, right sides together, as listed below.
    A and B: 2 pairs
    A and C: 4 pairs
    A and D: 4 pairs
    B and C: 2 pairs
    B and D: 5 pairs
    C and D: 4 pairs

2 Mark a diagonal line from corner to corner on the wrong side of the lighter fabric in each pair. Stitch each pair of squares together, sewing ¼" from the diagonal line on each side.

Mark.   Stitch.

3 Press the squares flat as sewn, and then cut each pair of squares in half on the marked line. Trim the dog-ears (corners) and press the units open, pressing the seam allowances toward the darker fabric. Trim each unit to 4" x 4". You will have 42 half-square-triangle units. Reserve two A/D and two C/D units for the pieced backing. One A/D and one C/D unit will be left over.

Cut.   Press open.

Assembling the Quilt Top

1 Arrange the plain 4" squares and the half-square-triangle units in 13 rows of 13 units each, referring to the quilt assembly diagram on page 20. Correct placement and orientation of each unit is essential to form the O shapes in the quilt layout.

2 Sew the units together into rows, pressing the seam allowances open to reduce bulk later. (Or press to one side, if you prefer.)

3 Sew the rows together, pinning at all seam intersections. Press the seam allowances open.

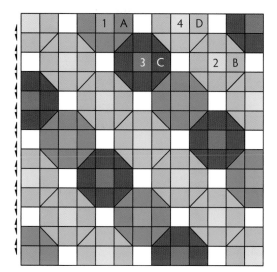

Quilt assembly

Assembling the Backing

To coordinate with the quilt front, Shea made an additional pieced block and set it into a pieced quilt backing. You can follow her lead for a fun quilt backing, or use a plain backing if you're in a hurry!

Additional Cutting

From the backing fabric, cut:
1 rectangle, 32" x 53"
1 rectangle, 10" x 53"
1 rectangle, 9" x 11"

From the remainder of fabric A, cut:
1 strip, 11" x 34"

Width Wise

Cut the two 53" lengths of backing fabric by splitting the fabric lengthwise into approximately 10" and 32" sections. If the fabric is a bit less than 42" wide, the backing will be slightly smaller than the batting, but it will still be large enough to finish the quilt. It's okay to include the selvages in these width measurements, as they will be trimmed away before the quilt binding is added.

Piecing the Back

1 Using the reserved half-square-triangle units, fabric D squares, and fabric 4 square, assemble one block.

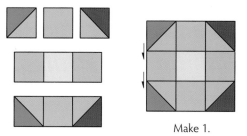

Make 1.

2 Sew the fabric A strip to the side of the block with A/D units and add the 9" x 11" rectangle of fabric C to the opposite side of the block. Pin and then sew the long fabric C pieces to the top and bottom of the pieced strip as shown. Press the seam allowances away from the pieced block.

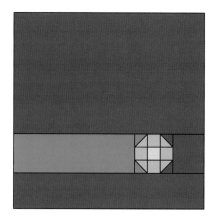

Pieced quilt back

Finishing the Quilt

For more information on finishing techniques, go to ShopMartingale.com/HowtoQuilt for free illustrated instructions.

1 Prepare the quilt backing.

2 Layer the quilt top, batting, and backing; baste the layers together.

3 Hand or machine quilt the center of the quilt as desired.

4 Trim the backing and batting even with the quilt top, and then use the fabric C 2¼"-wide strips to bind the edges of the quilt. Add a label and sleeve if desired.

Tiny Bits

If you're like Rebecca, you know several people who are expecting and you'd like to make a quilt for each of them. This quilt is both cheerful and quick to stitch, making it the perfect choice for every expected baby.

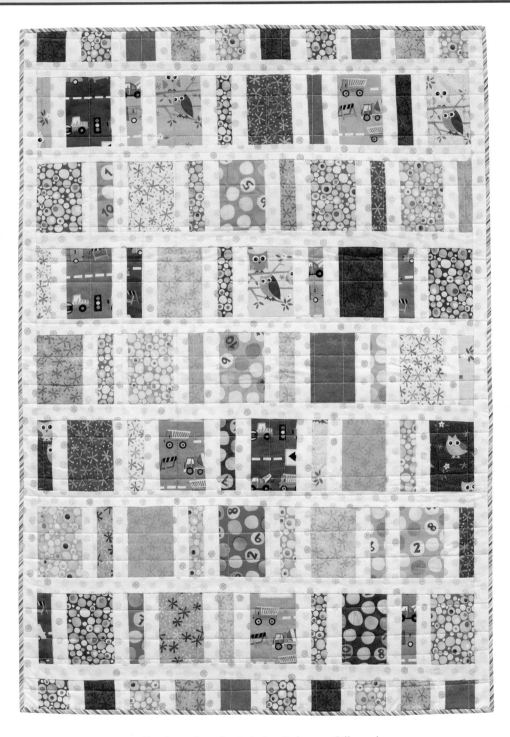

Designed and made by Rebecca Silbaugh

Quilt size: 31½" x 44" • **Block size:** 5" x 4½"

Materials

Yardage is based on 42"-wide fabric unless noted otherwise.

1 yard of light print for blocks, sashing, and border
40 assorted print charm squares, 5" x 5", for blocks and border
⅓ yard of diagonal stripe for binding
1⅔ yards of fabric for backing
36" x 50" piece of batting

Cutting

Measurements include ¼"-wide seam allowances.

From *each of 35* assorted 5" squares, cut:
1 rectangle, 1½" x 5" (35 total)
1 rectangle, 3½" x 5" (35 total; this piece will be left after cutting the previous piece, so you don't really have to cut anything)

From *each of the remaining 5* assorted 5" squares, cut:
4 squares, 2½" x 2½" (20 total)

From the light print, cut:
20 strips, 1½" x 42"; crosscut *10 of the strips* into:
    63 rectangles, 1½" x 5"
    22 rectangles, 1½" x 2½"

From the diagonal stripe, cut:
4 strips, 2¼" x 42"

Making the Blocks

1 Sew a light 1½" x 5" rectangle to each print 1½" x 5" rectangle along the long edges. Press the seam allowances toward the assorted rectangle. Make 35.

Make 35.

2 Sew a different print 3½" x 5" rectangle to each unit from step 1. Press the seam allowances toward the large rectangle. Make 35 blocks, each measuring 5½" x 5".

Make 35.

Assembling the Quilt Top

1 Refer to the quilt assembly diagram on page 23 to lay out the blocks in seven rows of five blocks and four light 1½" x 5" rectangles each, rotating the blocks so the large and small assorted rectangles alternate from row to row. Rearrange the blocks as needed until you're satisfied with the color placement. Sew the blocks and rectangles in each row together. Press the seam allowances toward the blocks.

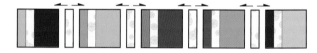

Make 7.

2 Measure the length of the pieced rows; determine the average of these measurements. Trim eight light 1½"-wide strips to the average length. Alternately sew the light sashing strips and block rows together, beginning and ending with a sashing strip. Press the seam allowances toward the sashing strips.

3 Measure the length of the quilt top through the middle and near both edges; determine the average of these measurements. Trim the two remaining light 1½"-wide strips to the average length. Sew the side border strips to the sides of the quilt top. Press the seam allowances toward the quilt center.

4 Sew a light 1½" x 2½" rectangle to one edge of each print 2½" square. Press the seam allowances toward the squares. Make 20.

Make 20.

5 Sew 10 of the pieced units end to end, alternating the light and print fabrics. Add a light 1½" x 2½" rectangle to the assorted-print end of the row. Make two pieced border strips.

Make 2.

6 Sew pieced border strips to the top and bottom of the quilt top. Press the seam allowances toward the quilt center.

Finishing the Quilt

For more information on finishing techniques, go to ShopMartingale.com/HowtoQuilt for free illustrated instructions.

1 Prepare the quilt backing.

2 Layer the quilt top, batting, and backing; baste the layers together.

3 Hand or machine quilt as desired.

4 Trim the backing and batting even with the quilt top, and then use the striped 2¼"-wide strips to bind the edges of the quilt. Add a label and sleeve if desired.

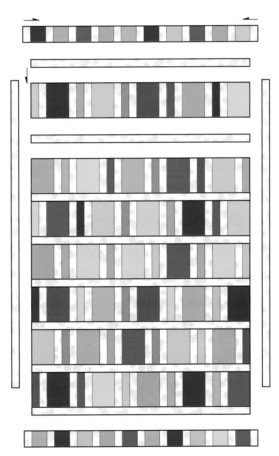

Quilt assembly

Ice Cream Swirl

This quilt block looks like simple squares pieced together, but it has a partially sewn seam thrown in for a twist. Challenge yourself—once you get the hang of the technique, this baby quilt can be pieced in a weekend or even a day!

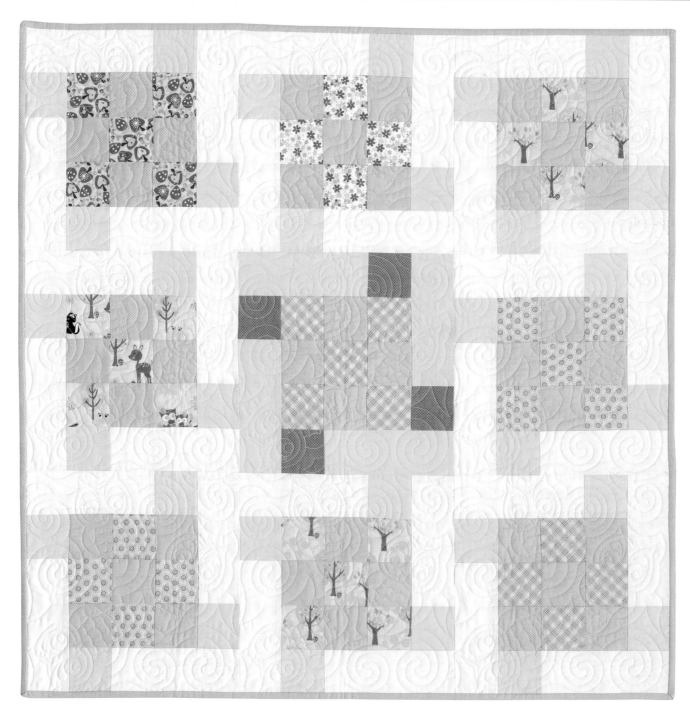

Designed and pieced by Victoria L. Eapen; machine quilted by Al Kuthe

Quilt size: 38" x 38" • **Block size:** 12½" x 12½"

Materials

Yardage is based on 42"-wide fabric.

⅔ yard of light solid for blocks

⅔ yard of green print for blocks and binding

⅛ yard or fat eighth *each* of 5 assorted pink prints for blocks

½ yard of yellow print for blocks

⅛ yard or fat eighth of red print for center block

2½ yards of fabric for backing

44" x 44" square of batting

Cutting

Measurements include ¼"-wide seam allowances.

From the green print, cut:

4 strips, 3" x 42"; crosscut into 40 squares, 3" x 3"

4 strips, 2¼" x 42"

From the 5 assorted pink prints, cut a *total* of:

5 *sets* of 5 matching squares, 3" x 3"

4 *sets* of 4 matching squares, 3" x 3"

From the yellow print, cut:

4 strips, 3" x 42"; crosscut into:

    32 squares, 3" x 3"

    4 rectangles, 3" x 8"

From the light solid, cut:

7 strips, 3" x 42"; crosscut into 32 rectangles, 3" x 8"

From the red print, cut:

4 squares, 3" x 3"

Making the Blocks

1 Arrange five green 3" squares and four matching pink 3" squares into three horizontal rows as shown. Sew the squares in each row together. Press the seam allowances toward the pink squares. Sew the rows together to make a nine-patch unit. Press the seam allowances toward the middle row. Repeat to make a total of four units.

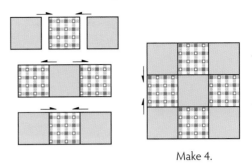

Make 4.

2 Arrange five matching pink 3" squares and four green 3" squares into three horizontal rows as shown. Sew the squares in each row together and press the seam allowances toward the green squares. Sew the rows together to make a nine-patch unit. Press the seam allowances toward the middle row. Repeat to make a total of five units.

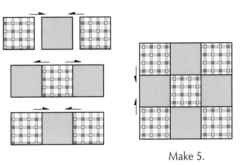

Make 5.

3 Sew a yellow 3" square to one end of each light 3" x 8" rectangle. Press the seam allowances toward the yellow squares.

Make 32.

4 Repeat step 3 with the red squares and yellow rectangles.

Make 4.

5 Partially sew a yellow rectangle unit from step 4 to the right-hand edge of a nine-patch unit from step 2. Begin at the lower-right corner of the nine-patch unit and sew two-thirds of the rectangle to the unit; backstitch and remove the unit from your machine. Press the seam allowances toward the rectangle. Sew another yellow rectangle unit to the bottom of the nine-patch unit. Continue adding the rectangle units to each side of the nine-patch unit, working clockwise. After you've added the last rectangle, complete the first seam to finish the center block. The completed block should measure 13" x 13".

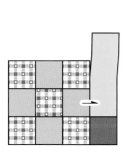
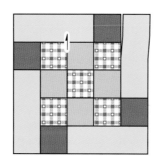
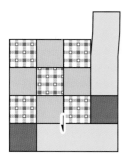
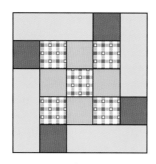

Make 1.

6 Repeat step 5 with the remaining nine-patch units from steps 1 and 2 and the light rectangle units from step 3.

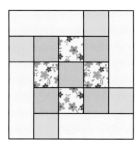
Make 4.

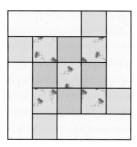
Make 4.

Assembling the Quilt Top

Arrange the blocks into three horizontal rows of three blocks each, placing the block with the yellow rectangles in the center of the layout as shown. Sew the blocks in each row together. Press the seam allowances in alternating directions from row to row. Sew the rows together. Press the seam allowances in one direction.

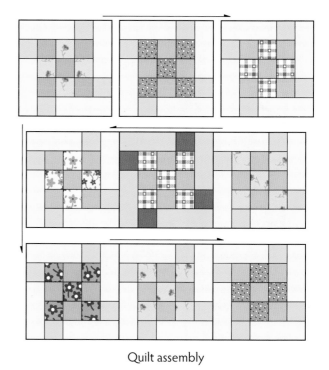

Quilt assembly

Finishing the Quilt

For more information on finishing techniques, go to ShopMartingale.com/HowtoQuilt for free illustrated instructions.

1 Prepare the quilt backing.

2 Layer the quilt top, batting, and backing; baste the layers together.

3 Hand or machine quilt as desired.

4 Trim the backing and batting even with the quilt top, and then use the green 2¼"-wide strips to bind the edges of your quilt. Add a label and sleeve if desired.

Penny Lane

To make this fun quilt, Sue simply sewed a big Four Patch block, cut it up, and sewed it back together again! You can use any Layer Cake bundle, or cut your own 10" squares.

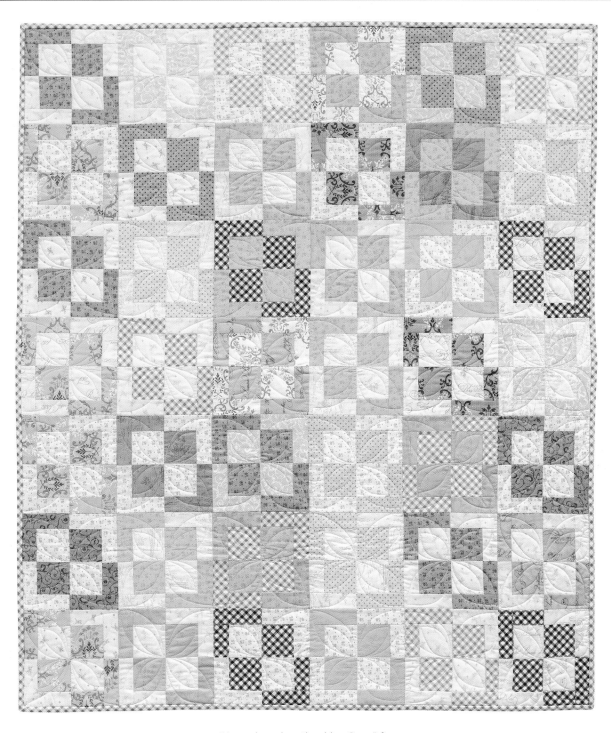

Pieced and quilted by Sue Pfau

Quilt size: 48½" x 56½" • **Block size:** 8" x 8"

Materials

Yardage is based on 42"-wide fabric, unless noted otherwise.

42 assorted squares, 10" x 10", for blocks
½ yard of blue-check for binding
3¼ yards of fabric for backing
57" x 65" piece of batting

Cutting

From *each* of the 10" squares, cut:
4 squares, 5" x 5" (168 total)

From the blue check, cut:
6 strips, 2½" x 42"

Piecing the Blocks

1 Select two contrasting pairs of matching 5" squares. Sew the squares together into a four-patch unit. Press the seam allowances toward the darker fabric.

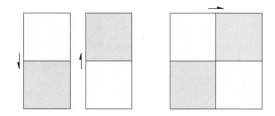

2 Cut 1¾"-wide strips off opposite sides of the four-patch unit in the order shown. You will be left with a 6" x 6" four-patch unit. Set the longer trimmed pieces aside for step 3 and the shorter ones for step 4.

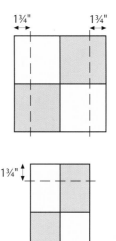

3 Trim the longer strips so they measure 4¼" on each side of the center seam. (8½" total length).

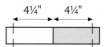

4 Sew the shorter 1¾"-wide strips back onto the top and bottom of the block, rotating the strips so that contrasting fabrics are joined. Press the seam allowances toward the center of the block. Sew the longer strips to the sides of the block. Press the seam allowances toward the left side of the block. The finished block should measure 8½" square; trim if necessary. If you trim the block, be sure to keep the middle seam at 4¼" on your ruler.

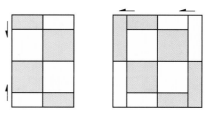

5 Repeat steps 1–4 to make a total of 42 blocks.

Assembling the Quilt Top

1 Arrange the blocks in seven horizontal rows of six blocks each, referring to the quilt assembly diagram on page 29. Sue laid out the blocks so the darker corners are always in the upper-left and lower-right corners. Rotate the blocks 180° as needed so that the seam allowances will butt against each other nicely.

2 Sew the blocks together into rows. Press the seam allowances in opposite directions from row to row. Join the rows. Press the seam allowances in the same direction.

Finishing the Quilt

For more information on finishing techniques, go to ShopMartingale.com/HowtoQuilt for free illustrated instructions.

1 Prepare the quilt backing.

2 Layer the quilt top, batting, and backing; baste the layers together.

3 Hand or machine quilt as desired.

4 Trim the backing and batting even with the quilt top, and then use the blue-check 2½"-wide strips to bind the edges of the quilt. Add a label and sleeve if desired.

Quilt assembly

Sweet Cheeks

This is the perfect go-to baby quilt when you need a shower gift in a jiffy. It's cute for both boys and girls, comes together quickly, and is oh-so sweet.

Designed and pieced by Rachel Griffith; quilted by Darla Padilla

Quilt size: 36½" x 36½"

Materials

Yardage is based on 42"-wide fabric unless noted otherwise.

10 fat eighths (9" x 21") of assorted prints for small block and rectangles
2 fat quarters (18" x 21") of assorted prints for large block
¾ yard of aqua print for large block and binding
1 scrap, at least 5" x 5", of print for small block
2½ yards of fabric for backing
41" x 41" piece of batting

Cutting

From 1 fat quarter, cut:
1 square, 8½" x 8½"

From the remaining fat quarter, cut:
2 strips, 4½" x 8½"
2 strips, 4½" x 16½"

From the print scrap, cut:
1 square, 4½" x 4½"

From *each of 8* fat eighths, cut:
1 strip, 6½" x 12½" (8 total)

From 1 fat eighth, cut:
2 strips, 2½" x 4½"
2 strips, 2½" x 8½"

From the remaining fat eighth, cut:
2 strips, 2½" x 8½"
2 strips, 2½" x 12½"

From the aqua print, cut:
2 strips, 4½" x 16½"
2 strips, 4½" x 24½"
4 strips, 2¼" x 42"

Making the Large Block

1 Sew the assorted 4½" x 8½" strips to opposite sides of the 8½" square. Press the seam allowances toward the strips. Sew the matching 4½" x 16½" strips to the top and bottom edges of the unit. Press the seam allowances toward the just-added strips.

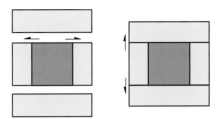

2 Sew the aqua 4½" x 16½" strips to opposite sides of the center unit. Press the seam allowances toward the aqua strips. Sew the aqua 4½" x 24½" strips to the top and bottom edges to complete the block. Press the seam allowances toward the just-added strips.

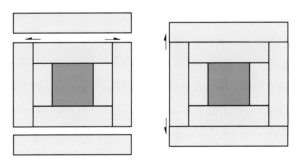

Making the Small Block

1 Sew the assorted 2½" x 4½" strips to opposite sides of the 4½" square. Press the seam allowances toward the strips. Sew the matching 2½" x 8½" strips to the top and bottom edges of the unit. Press the seam allowances toward the just-added strips.

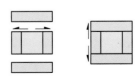

2 Sew the assorted 2½" x 8½" strips to opposite sides of the center unit. Press the seam allowances toward the just-added strips. Sew the matching 2½" x 12½" strips to the top and bottom edges to complete the block. Press the seam allowances toward the just-added strips.

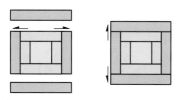

Assembling the Quilt Top

1 Join four assorted 6½" x 12½" rectangles side by side to make a rectangular unit. Press the seam allowances in one direction. Repeat to make a second rectangular unit.

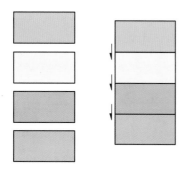

2 Lay out the large block, small block, and the two rectangular units as shown in the quilt assembly diagram above right.

3 Sew the blocks and units together into rows. Press the seam allowances toward the blocks. Then join the rows to complete the quilt top. Press the seam allowances in one direction.

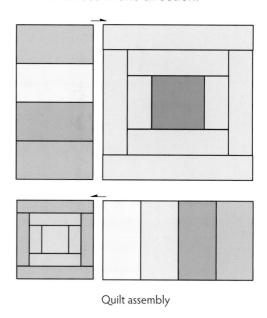

Quilt assembly

Finishing the Quilt

For more information on finishing techniques, go to ShopMartingale.com/HowtoQuilt for free illustrated instructions.

1 Prepare the quilt backing.

2 Layer the quilt top, batting, and backing; baste the layers together.

3 Hand or machine quilt as desired.

4 Trim the backing and batting even with the quilt top, and then use the aqua 2¼"-wide strips to bind the edges of the quilt. Add a label and sleeve if desired.